MW00813441

Progressions
the art of Jon Foster

This book is dedicated to Melissa Ferreira.

Special thanks to
Rick Berry, Millie Foster, Carol Grabbert, Lars Grant-West,
Debra Page-Trim, and Christopher Reilly.

Without you, this book wouldn't exist.

Introduction by Christopher P. Reilly
Design, Layout, and Production by Page Trim Design
Production Assistance by Wayne Barrett and Philip Reed
Proofreading and Print Buying by Monica Stephens

Editor in Chief ✠ Steve Jackson
Creative Director ✠ Philip Reed
Sales Manager ✠ Ross Jepson

www.cartouchepress.com
www.jonfoster.com

ISBN 1-55634-626-3

1 2 3 4 5 6 7 8 9 10

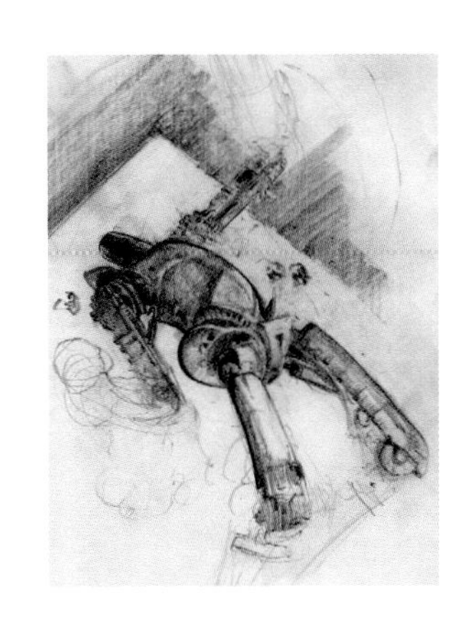

ALIENS VS PREDATOR
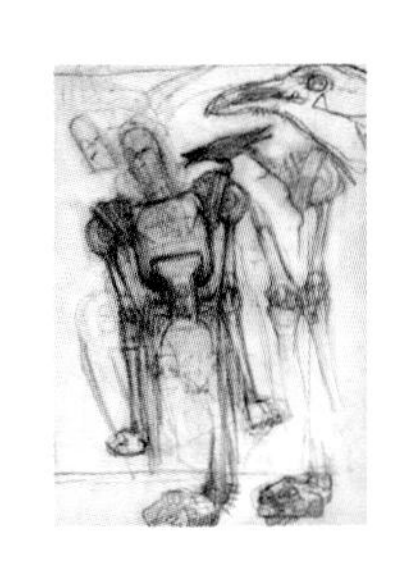
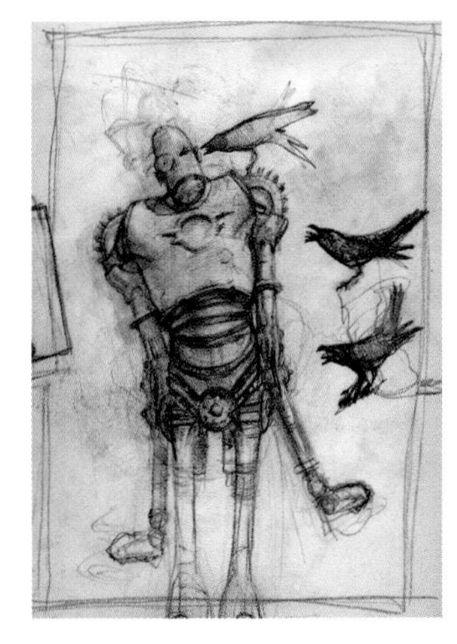
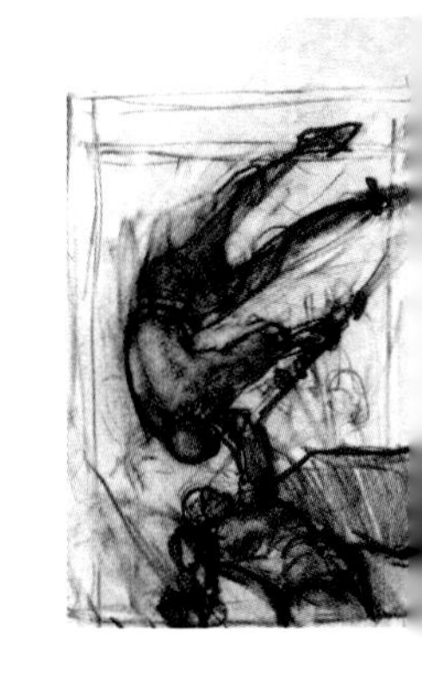

When I was asked to write an introduction to *Progressions*, I was honored to say the least. Jon Foster is more than just a wonderful artist – of whom I am a fan – he's also a great guy, good friend, and a fellow Rondo "the Creeper" Hatton enthusiast.

There is always a textured sense of character in his paintings that transcends the stroke of the brush, and digs deep beneath the painted surface. I look at the Twi'lek girl, Aayla Secura, immortalized on the covers of issues 33 to 35 of the ongoing *DHC Star Wars* comic-book title, as a perfect example. Before Jon put brush to canvas, all we knew of this race was that they had gruesomely ugly "tentacled" heads, and were screeching victims or backup singers in weird, Muppet bands. Without Mr. Foster's stunning renditions of this Twi'lek Jedi warrior, we would still have the image of these tragic fodder beings, and nothing more. But suddenly, we have an Aayla Secura who moves with a fluid, mythical grace that would have given Gustav Klimt cause to take notice, a presence that exudes beauty as much as it does danger. Jon not only gave a silly, throwaway, bordering-on-the-pathetic character presence, he somehow managed to empower her.

I think, above all, that is where Jon's strength lies as an artist. He gets deep inside what he's painting and gives it a purposeful sense of being. The work speaks in a language that both the eye and the intellect can savor. Proof of this would be the addition of Aayla Secura to an upcoming film – with Jon's covers as the inspiration and reason for her inclusion. As a big nerd, I'm probably more excited for Jon than he is for himself.

Jon doesn't think he's all that spectacular. I believe he's perched on a precipice of greatness, and the only thing holding him back from joining the highest ranks of his contemporaries is self-effacement. The very reason you're reading my take on Jon Foster is that he doesn't feel comfortable talking about his work. I imagine that his lack of bravado probably defines him as a person. He's incredibly gifted, and is climbing the ladder of recognition, but at heart, he's just this nice guy who loves what he does.

I would be remiss if I neglected to mention Jon's charming and beautiful wife, Melissa Ferreira. Mel's the anchor to his ship, a gifted artist as well as his primary model. Jon probably would not exist, as we know him, without their bond.

My working experience with Jon has been limited due to his busy schedule, but it has been rewarding. Jon illustrated the cover for my book *The Comical Tragedy of Punch and Judy,* and he one-upped my partner (the also brilliantly gifted) Darron Laessig and myself. A story that had taken us three years and 40-some-odd pages to tell has somehow been summed up in a single conception by Jon with his stunning painting. If that sounds a bit gushing, flip to page 59 and stare at the guy with the big nose and funny hat, and try to imagine what Mr. Foster could accomplish with 32 pages, several hundred sequential panels, and some dialogue.

In my world of fanciful bliss, Jon would be putting the final touches on his first graphic novel, and it would have a title like *Big Honking Robot Stories*. If Jon never gets around to exposing the world to this sequential masterpiece, I'd be more than happy, and honored, to write *Big Honking Robot Stories* for him . . . but I think he'd do a better job. If you don't believe me, check out the venerable 'bot battalion on the pages that follow this introduction, and judge for yourself.

Welcome to the works of Jon Foster; welcome to *Progressions*.

– Christopher P. Reilly

Mopiebot
Oil on board
27" x 40"

Hunter #8
Oil on board/digital
20" x 22"

The Flea
Digital

Mechanic
Acrylic, oil, and colored pencil on board
10" x 14"

Fish and Chips
Digital

Star Wars #34
Oil on canvas
30" x 40"

Body Tanks
Digital

Hanging Around
Digital

Diesel
Digital

Big Fight Scene Take 93
Digital

WAREHOUSE

Hunter #7
Oil on board/digital
27″ x 39″

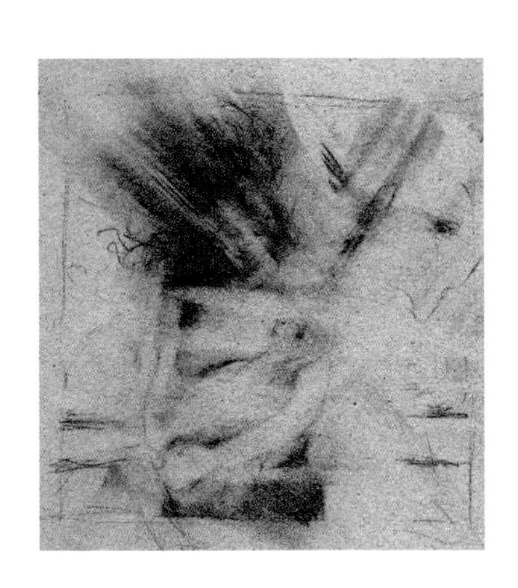

Vader vs. Maul
Oil on board/digital
12" x 18"

Bloodtide
Oil on board/digital
21″ x 36″

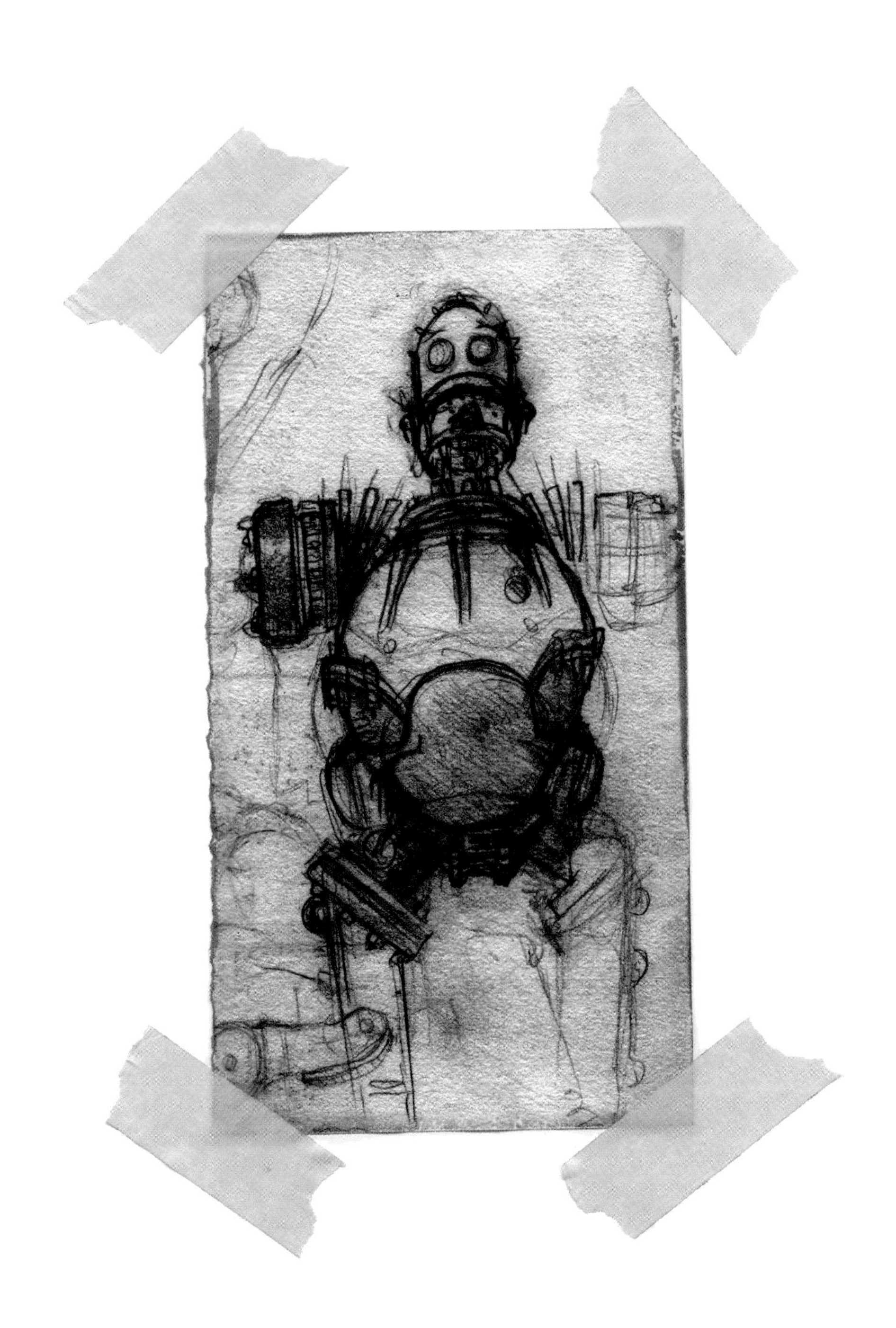

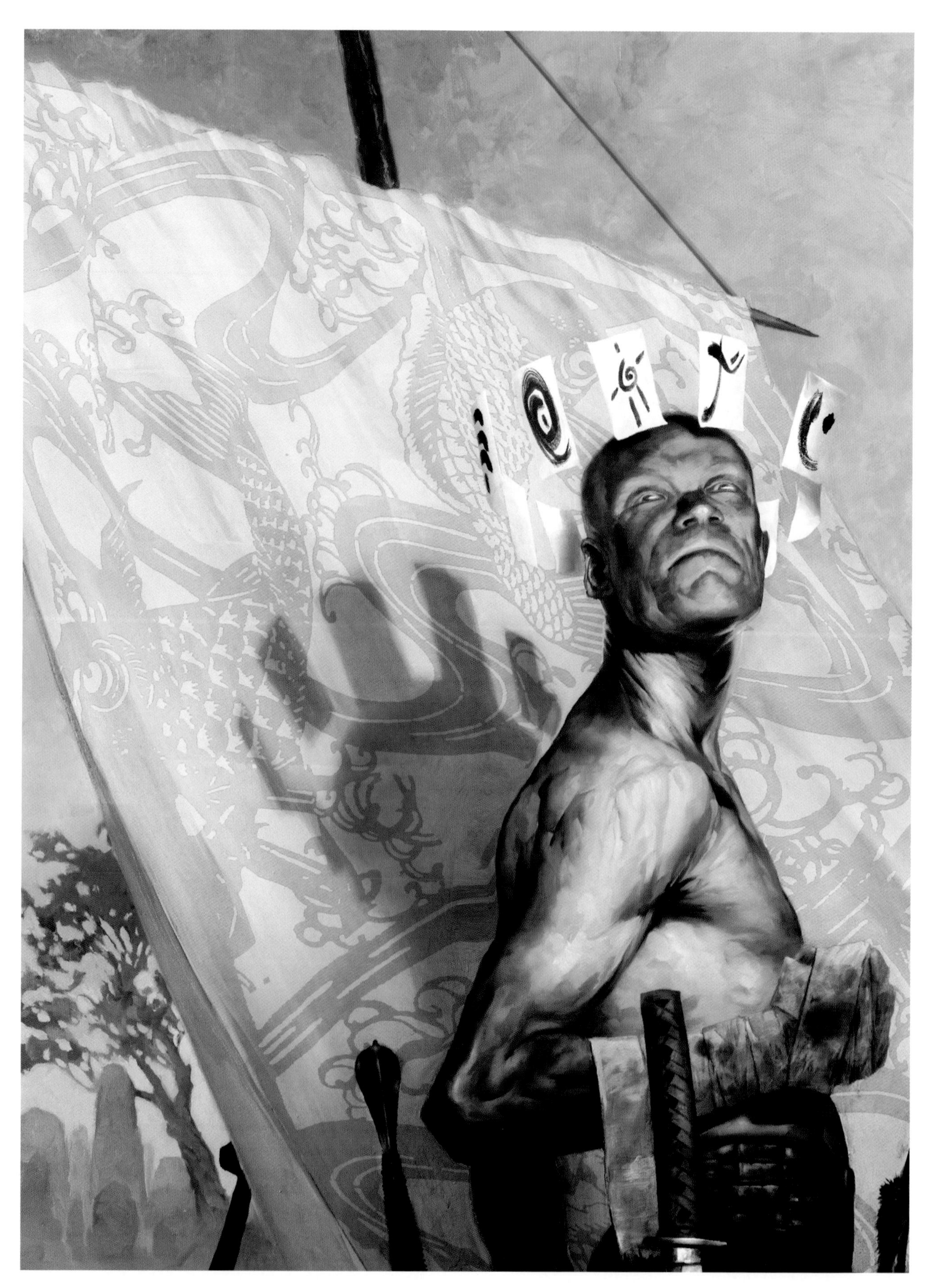

Dragon
Oil on canvas/digital
30″ x 40″

Stonehead
Oil on board/digital
30" x 40"

Core
Digital

Mothership
Oil on board/digital
18″ x 24″

J·F
R·B

The wonder of including the computer in my process is the ability to try endless variations on a theme and, if they don't work out, Command Z is just a click away. Oddly, this sense of experimentation helps me in my approach to oil painting. As I am used to revising compositions digitally, I feel they can be changed in the oil paint, too. It's more difficult and time-consuming, but I still do them. My usual process is sketch, paint with oils on large board, revamp the composition in the computer, and paint again.

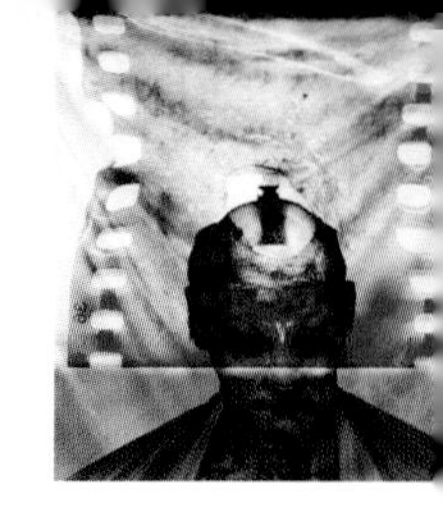

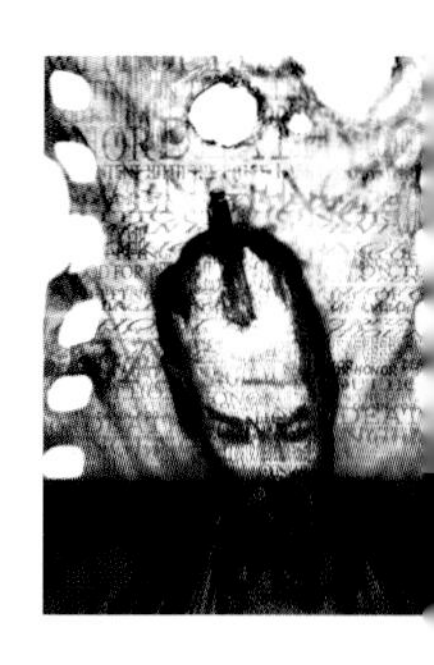

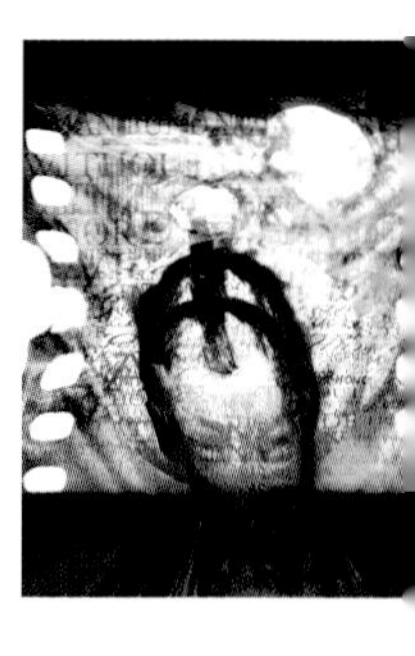

Private Screening
Digital

Sex With a Wrench
Digital
art in collaboration with Rick Berry

Star Wars #39
Oil on canvas/digital

Working on the covers for this *Star Wars* series was a joy. The interior art by Jan Dureschema filled the pages with excitement, intrigue, and excellent storytelling. Her pencils were sent to me for reference, and immediately upon viewing them, myriad possibilities for paintings formed in my imagination. But on this occasion, there was one particular panel of Jan's that I knew I wanted to do. With just a little revision, I set to work and painted one of my favorite covers in the series.

Star Wars #35
Oil on canvas/digital
30" x 40"

If I had time to paint just robots, that's all my work would be – robots! They're iconic, like the idea of chair or house. They are us in disguise, superpowered, cold and warm, young and old, symbols for us to ponder what makes us human. Do the parts add to the personality of the robot? Define it? Maybe certain robots were created by other machines, not manufactured by humans but somehow evolving on their own so that none would ever be alike. Their junkyard-assemblage appearance is their individuality. In my mind, bad-guy robots are replicable and identical. I'm also fascinated by the aesthetic of heavy industrial machinery with its cast-iron chunky bits. I find myself entranced by rusty old tractors and water towers with textures of deterioration, whether they're perfectly functioning or high-tech. I love the possibilities inherent in the making of the machine and its change over time.

Hunter #10
Oil on canvas/digital
22" x 22"

Cliffhanger
Oil on paper/digital
12.5" x 16.5"

This project was great fun. I had the good fortune of having an excellent art director, Paul Hanchette, who gave me free rein on the portraits. With support and prodding from fellow artist Rick Berry, I discovered what could happen by exploring pencil marks on paper instead of forcing a fleeting vision from my mind's eye into objectivity. The results were far more inspirational to my overall approach to art-making than these illustrations alone could convey. I learned that I should push and pull images from their very beginning, stay open to unknown possibilities, and fearlessly make changes. I must feel passion and conviction in every piece and for the process of painting overall.

Alternity Portraits
Digital

Clean Murder
Digital

Sketchbooks are works of art, though I admit that I don't usually feel that way about my own. I could look at other artists' sketchbooks all day. I like seeing the many interpretations of life observed or the paths of a whimsical mind wandering. There's a wealth of reaching, searching, and unrestrained experimentation in journals that shows creativity beyond the polish of finished images. I have a constant resource in my wife's sketchbooks. I sometimes look to their pages for ways of getting out of a worn track of thinking and to see another artist's approach that's completely different from how I might go about a sketch.

Luck was with me on this piece. The art director and I wanted to step to the left of the fantasy genre with this series of book covers. His colleagues didn't initially accept my preliminary sketch, but Jon Schindehette pushed for my strongly held vision. He's an art director who's willing to go beyond the familiar conventions of the trade (or even throw the rules out the window). Mind you, this painting is not so radically different from your typical fantasy book cover, but it still took a good deal of campaigning to bring it to press.

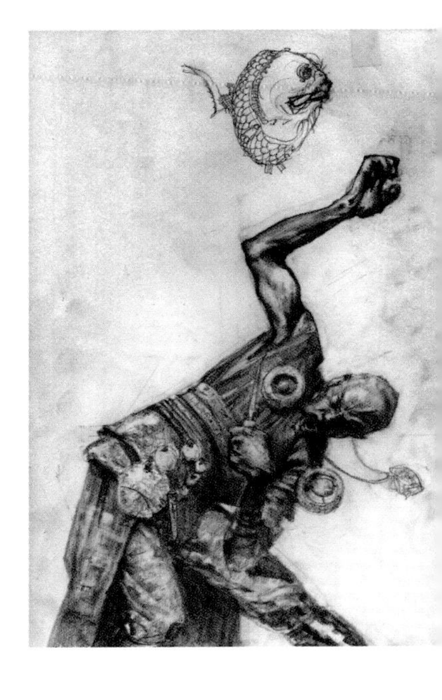

Magehound
Oil on board/digital
24″ x 48″

Floodgate
Oil on canvas/digital
30″ x 30″

Wizard Wars
Oil on canvas/digital
30″ x 30″

Catbot
Oil/digital
30″ x 40″

Desolation
Digital

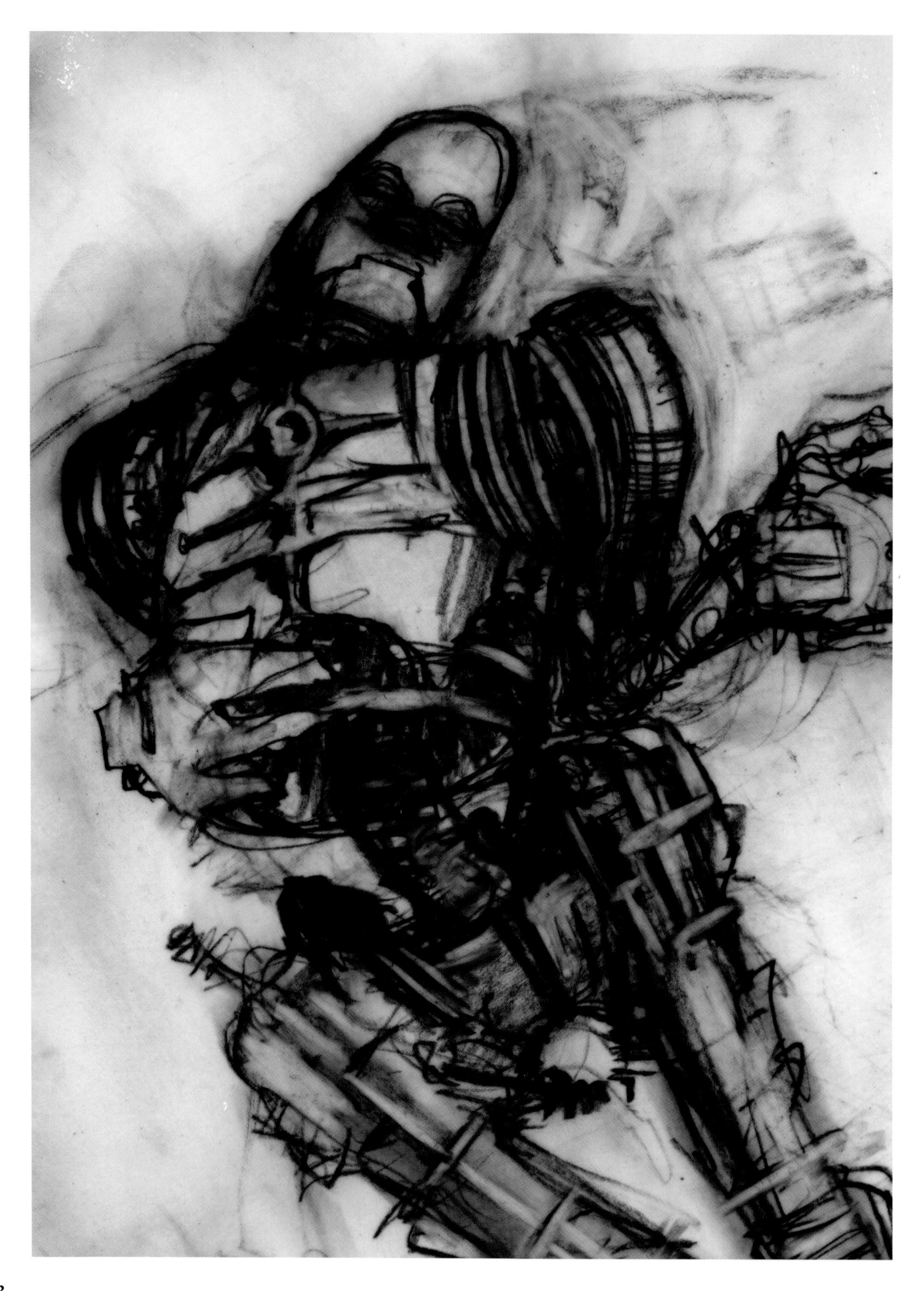

Blue (Star Wars #33)
Oil on board/digital
20" x 30"

Bubble Baby
Acrylic on board/digital
8″ x 8″

The Wolf
Digital

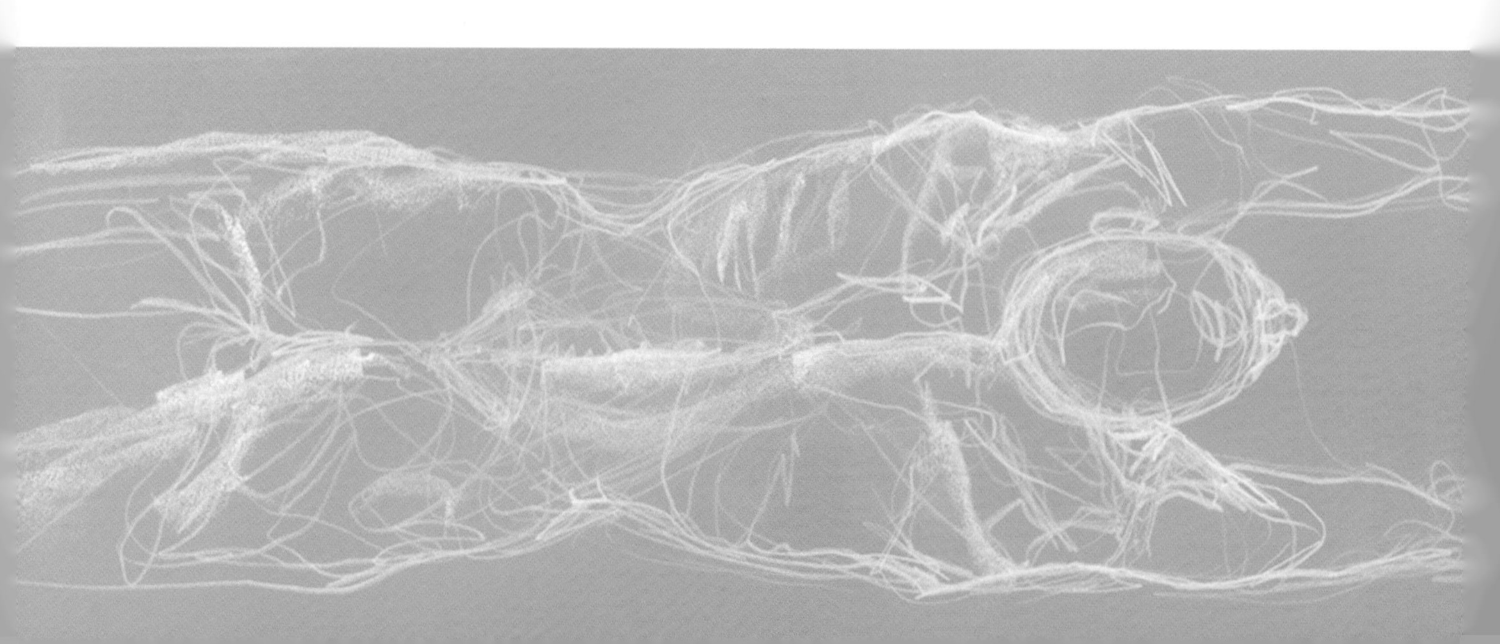

Punch
Acrylic on paper/digital
11″ x 17″

blue
bolt

Blue Bolt
Oil on board/digital
11″ x 17″

Big Fight Scene Take 3
Digital

Corum
Oil on board/digital
27″ x 39″

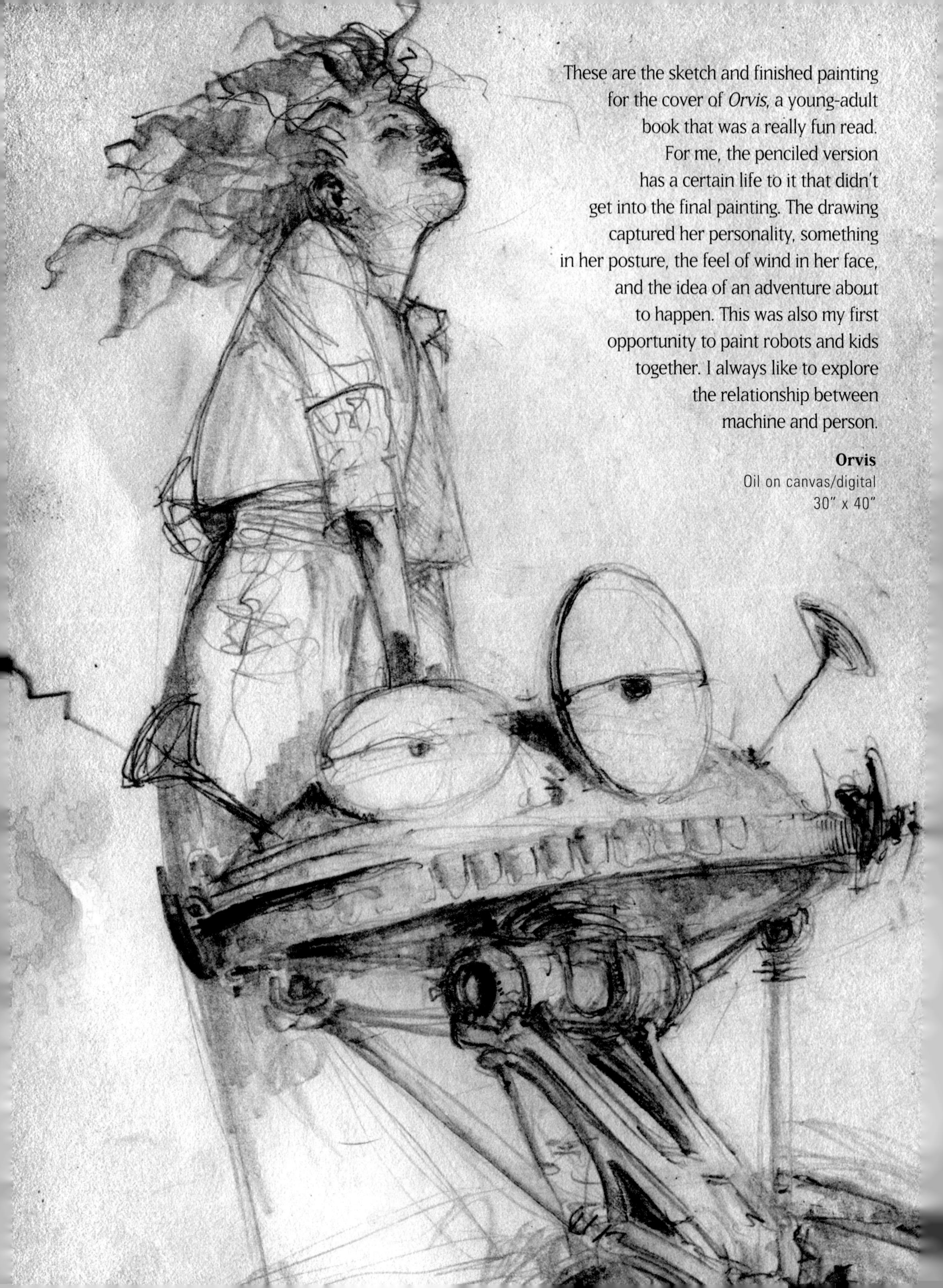

These are the sketch and finished painting for the cover of *Orvis*, a young-adult book that was a really fun read. For me, the penciled version has a certain life to it that didn't get into the final painting. The drawing captured her personality, something in her posture, the feel of wind in her face, and the idea of an adventure about to happen. This was also my first opportunity to paint robots and kids together. I always like to explore the relationship between machine and person.

Orvis
Oil on canvas/digital
30" x 40"

Klik
Oil on board
20" x 30"

Star Wars #31
Oil on board/digital
21.5" x 33"

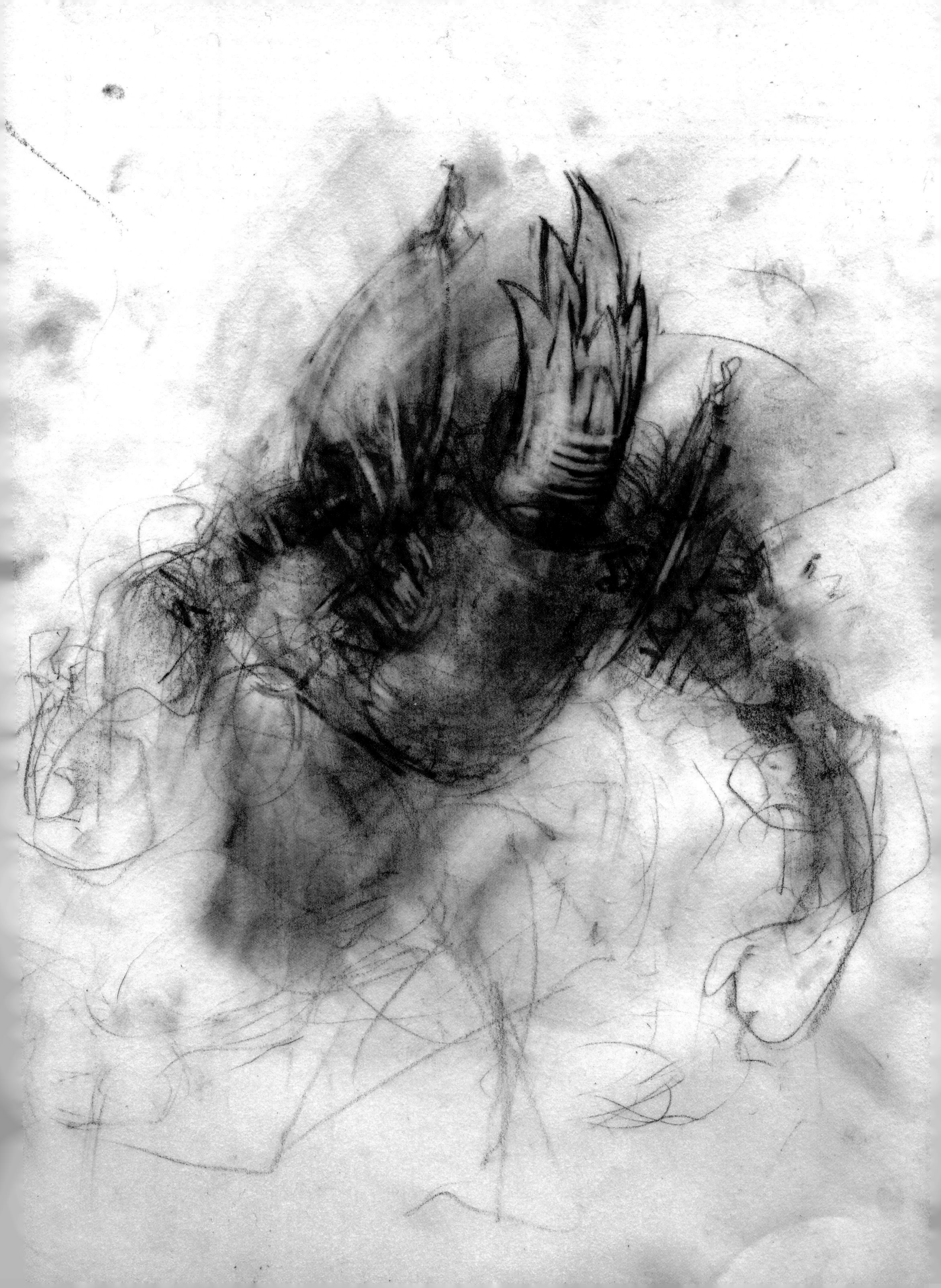

Star Wars #28
Oil on board/digital
20" x 30"

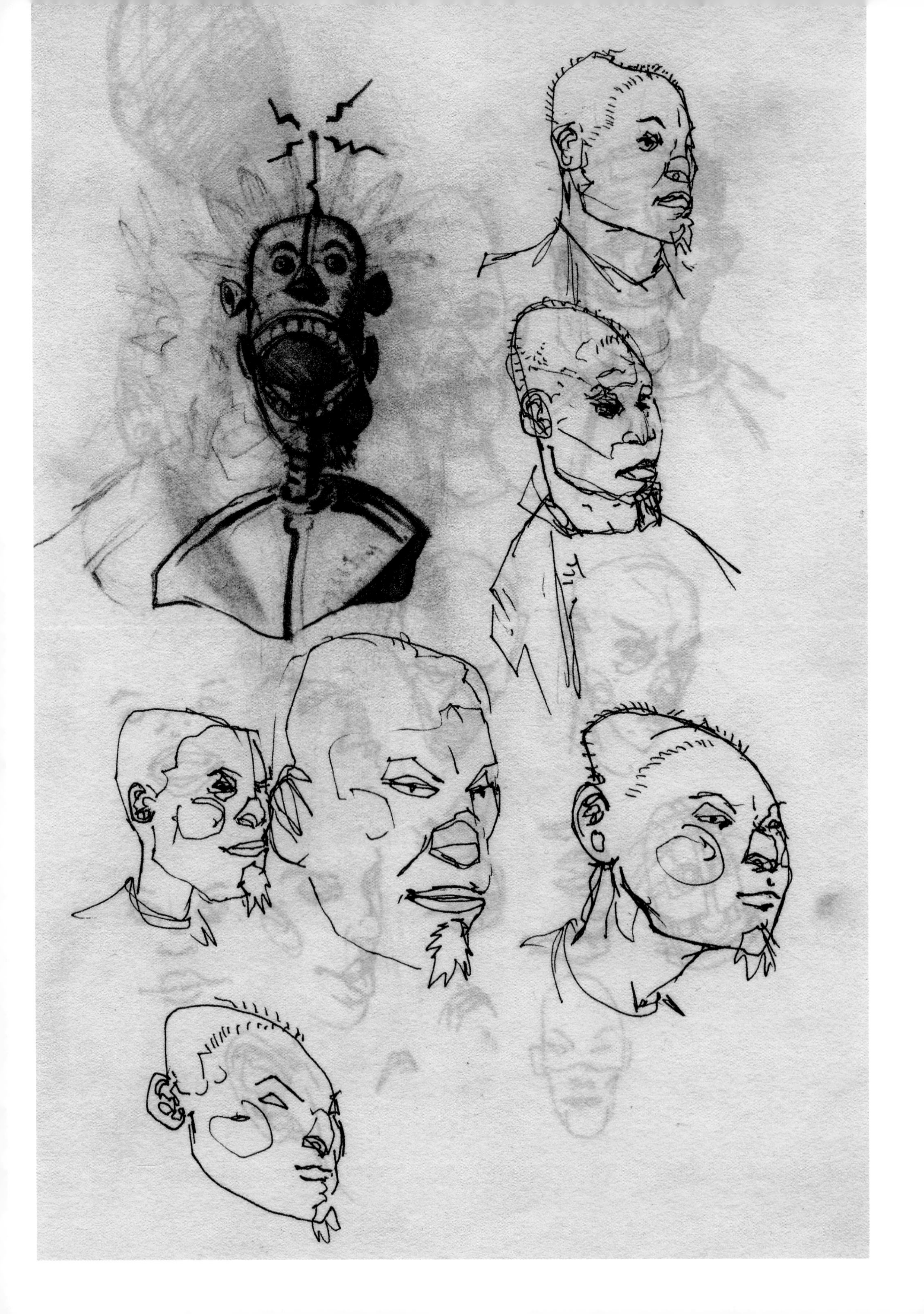

41861701
22A

Crowbot is a personal piece. Rick Berry suggested that I explore images with shapes and forms without human figures. Innovation would happen if I could avoid getting caught up in what I know about anatomy, what I think painters should know about it, or how they usually describe it. The exercise taught me to be more open with making marks and letting those loose gestural movements give birth to something else. Crowbot is what I found in the shapes and the texture of the paint itself. As it came into existence, I speculated on the relationship between animal and machine, crow and robot. Thematically, I keep returning to the contradiction between the machine and human form, the machine anthropomorphized, a lifeless being that is paradoxically animated by expression and personality.

Crowbot
Oil on board
24" x 40"

Dove
Digital

Sylune
Digital

Alustriel
Digital

Laeral
Digital

Quilue
Digital

Storm
Digital

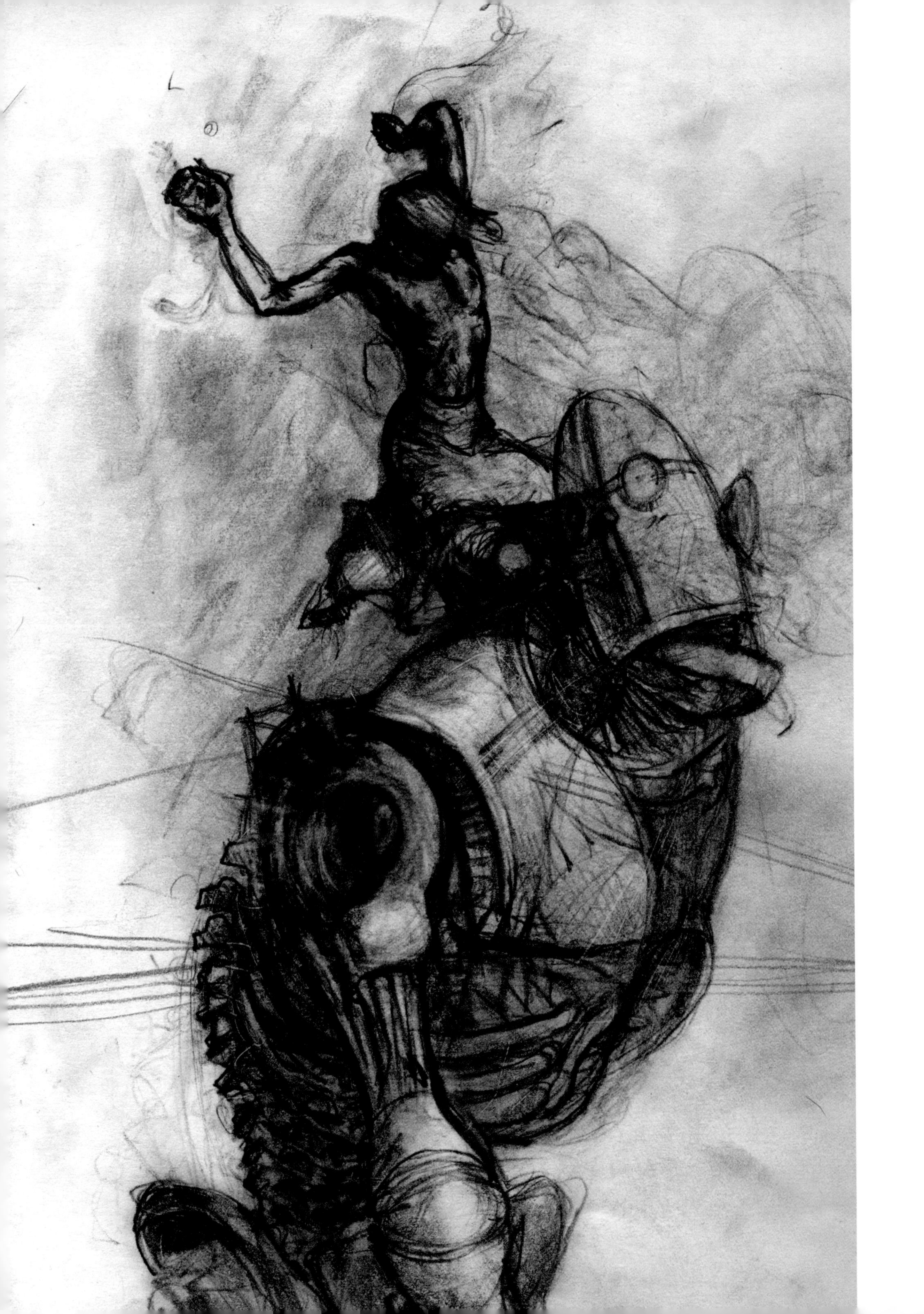